# Inspire, Inspiring, Inspired

## THE JOURNEY OF LIVING, LOVING & LEARNING

Mona-Lisa Fynn

Presentation by *BookLeaf Publishing*

Web: www.bookleafpub.com

E-mail: info@bookleafpub.com

ISBN: 9789358361193

First edition 2021

I dedicate this book to God, and my ghost writer, the Holy Spirit for not only inspiring me but also helping to turn my inspiration into written concepts.

I also want to say thank you to my mum, dad and brother who have always supported my endeavours and helped me become the person I am today

Also thank you to the friends who continue to motivate and inspire me in everything I do

This book wouldn't have been possible without any of you!

# Preface

For me, my interest in poetry stemmed
from boredom but quickly became a way
for me to express my thoughts and
feelings and was the outlet I never knew I
needed, helping me to catch my breath
when the world made it hard to

I never initially planned to share my
words so publicly but poetry inspires me
and it's my hope that my poetry will
inspire you

So someone said that they've loved seeing
how I've grown into myself and seem
much happier and it got me thinking –

I've been reflecting on the life of a
previous me whose self-esteem was
constantly shrinking

And I'm asking myself what changed?


The very essence of who you think you are
can evolve in what feels like the blink of
an eye - isn't that strange?

But nowhere near as strange as realising
you honestly didn't know yourself the
entire time and where some people might
see that as a shame I think that I'm just
taking pleasure now in understanding
what fills up the frame of this masterpiece
that is me


Before I used to hate the fact I didn't
understand myself but instead of giving
myself time to grow I tried to use the

people around me to uphold my created
sense of identity,

As if we weren't all insecure little girls just
trying to form ourselves into somewhat
functioning entities

And it broke me.

Back to square one with no clue who I
wanted to be,

It's no wonder back then I wasn't happy


So by now you're probably asking the
same question - what changed?

I guess life happened and it made analyse
the pieces of me that I wanted to hold on
to,

Being broken gave me a chance to work
out which parts were "faulty" and which
parts were true

And I'm not necessarily saying the faulty
parts were bad but they affected my
authenticity and left me with holes

Because if you've built yourself with
pieces that don't really fit, you can never
feel whole

Just because I like how a piece fits in
someone else's frame doesn't mean I
should try and make a similar thing fit in
mine

And that's why the whole comparison
thing doesn't work - we're all
fundamentally different in our design


So yes I have grown into myself, but it
definitely got worse before it improved,
And I really struggled when so many
things I thought I knew about myself were
disproved

They say "fake it 'til you make it" but that
can only get you so far,

At some point you have to question your
foundations or you'll keep breaking and
being left to count your scars

It's so important to recognise that your
own puzzle is inherently full of beauty

And you should see learning to love
yourself as a requisite duty

So when people praise me for learning to
define myself outside of what I can do for
others

I can only laugh when I think of how
many people I previously smothered

And what a change actually experiencing
happiness from constantly feeling numb
But that's growth and I know the younger
me is so proud of how far I've come

Yesterday I experienced my first ever heartbreak, it sounds crazy to say because love (and the lack thereof) is something I write about often, but this is a completely novel ache

I also learnt that anything but the purest most unadulterated version of love has the ability to leave you shattered, it's got me wondering why I thought the wrong things mattered and seriously praying that I don't make this a pattern

You see I didn't realise how wrong it was for me to hold on, that sometimes you might not feel ready but that doesn't mean it's not time to release the baton, and sometimes what you've been working so hard towards isn't what you need, even if you might feel attached after planting a seed

And part of me wants to tell you that love is a scam and that the moment you feel yourself falling you should run as fast as you can but it would be unfair for me to sell you the notion of never trusting a man, not only because that isn't me, but

also because how else will you find a love
that's true... so despite how I feel right
now, I know loving (the right person) isn't
the worst thing I could do

they say your first love is your first toxic
attachment I mean even he said it too

and I guess it takes really coming to your
senses to be able to face the truth,

saying that though I always knew that
something was wrong,

but it took me a while to realise fighting to
keep something isn't the only way to show
that you're strong



they say hurt people hurt people and that's
a cycle we knew well

and I still don't understand how I got
wrapped to the point I couldn't break free
even after the farewell,

and if I were to try and pinpoint the
toxicity, there would be a lengthy list of
both our tendencies

but if I had to pick my favourite weapon I
guess it was the emotional manipulation
for me

they say you live and you learn, I say
sometimes the lessons get delayed,

because sometimes things didn't actually
happen in the way that your memories
portrayed,

that's the thing about toxicity, it can make
you believe that anything that had thorns
was a rose, because no one wants to believe
that something simply painful is what
they chose


they say everything happens for a reason
but they also say everybody makes
mistakes,

and sometimes to learn the real lessons
pain is what it takes,

but even after the dreariest season, the sun
always shines again

In a world where nothing is a given,
gratitude really is paramount

And although it's not always easy to see,
look close and you'll find that blessings
still abound

And in a world that's so fast paced,
sometimes we're so busy that we don't
take time to realise

Things like the love of the people around
us or the beauty in every sunrise

They say there's a friend that sticks closer
than a brother and I have to agree,

the love from my friends is something
that's always been guaranteed,

it's not always easy to acknowledge when
someone has such a strong impact on your
life, in fact for me it's been scary

maybe that's why when it comes to letting
people get close I've always felt a little bit
wary...


I remember recently talking to an Uber
driver who was telling me about one of his
childhood friends,

And it made me stop and take time to
realise their value but I also won't pretend
-

Life gets busy and takes people down
varying lanes,

Which is part of growing up so I'll never
complain,

But what a pleasure to be reunited and in
knowing the love is still there,

That you might not have seen each other
for years but that they still care


And I'll be honest my friends, old and
"new" have made me the person I am
today,

and the love I have for them is something
I know my words just can't convey

But I will simply say I'm grateful to have
them in my life,

And I can't wait to see how we all
continue to thrive

It's better to fall short of your potential
than to stop short,

but the fear alone of failure seems to leave
us feeling distraught,

In a world where it seems like perfection is
synonymous with success,

not trying to reach our goals at all
seemingly hurts less


Having said this, if you're not confident in
yourself how can you expect anyone else
to be?

Because if you don't try how will you ever
know what you can achieve?

If you could just believe that there are
endless possibilities,

The world becomes your oyster and taking
risks becomes earlier than you first
perceived

This is your future so you have to take charge,

And don't forget to shoot for the moon, even if you miss you'll still land among the stars

You can be grateful to the ones who made you who you are,

But that doesn't negate the fact that relationships are hard...

Some people get busy and fail to make time,

Others are too busy but pretend everything's fine,

In life it's difficult to juggle everything so I have extreme respect to those who try,

But I'm learning not to negate people's balancing acts just because they're not the same as mine


I think I set up high expectations and feign surprise when people bail,

But I guess it's because I know I'm even harder on myself so in comparison those expectations pale,

Which begs the question, why am I repeatedly setting people up to "fail"?

I think a challenge is created when
balancing the notion that no one owes you
anything, and knowing what you deserve,

Because despite things not being set in
stone you should still know your worth

And bad past experiences can make this
even harder to navigate

But don't let that destroy the new
relationships you're trying to cultivate

Let's talk about cultivation - a process of
growing and sacrificing to reap something
worthwhile,

Sometimes pouring sweat and tears in
with no certainty that it'll end with a
smile

But still you strive

For what good is it to be alive with
nothing to show for it?

So we stomach the growing pains with
hope that they'll be to our benefit

And they often are,

Giving us worthy stories of how we got
our scars

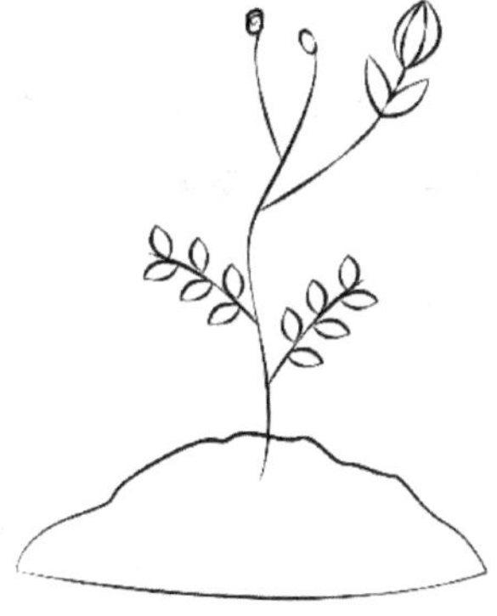

Have you ever felt the struggle of
conflicting beliefs?

For me the most common is about what
I'll achieve

Because I've learnt what it feels like to be
empty but concurrently full

And what it's like to be in alternate
directions pulled

It's a serious struggle going on a journey
when you're not sure of the destination,

Having multiple passions but knowing
you need divine revelation

And after getting that it feels like a new
journey begins, in the labour of love to
achieve those wins

The brooding stage of creating the perfect
conditions for your ideas to be birthed

Really does help you understand both their
& the struggle's worth

Dear younger me,

I know you must be confused about the
person I am today

Which isn't surprising as we've had many
passions along the way

Meaning we've never really been sure of
who we are or how we'll turn out

But let's be honest, something great was
birthed from our doubts

You never used to let anything deter you
from what you thought you wanted

Maybe that led you astray from time to
time, but generally I wish we were still
that dauntless,

There's a lot you will learn in the coming
years,

You'll shed tears, face losses, and develop
many fears,

I know you'd rather my spoilers just be the
highlights but you need to know you
pulled through,

And even despite those things, you not
only grew but you bloomed

It feels like I've come to another cross-
roads

And once again I have no clue where any
of the paths go

So I've been searching and part of me
thought that by now I'd know

But can you really call it searching when
you have no clue what you're in pursuit
of?


I guess I should find comfort in the fact
that not all who wander are lost

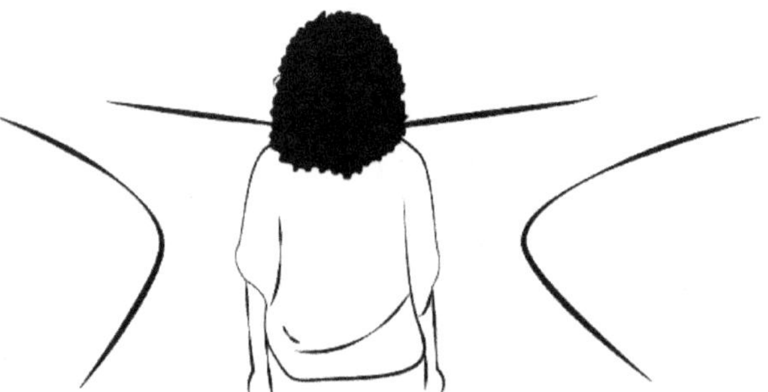

If there's one thing you need to know
about me, it's that no matter how much I
kid myself I'm a romantic,

Although I wouldn't say the "hopeless"
variety on account of the fact I'm also
pedantic,

Blame it on the hundreds of rom-coms I've
read but never fully believed,

Or maybe the fact that my heart
seemingly lives on my sleeve,

But for one reason or another as much as I
love love, its appeal has dwindled to me,

Maybe for fear of what will happen when
I find it, or maybe I'm just tired of writing
love poetry


Let's be real though, if everyone had to be
perfect before they fell in love, romance
would cease to exist,

And if you're looking to deploy the perfect
soldier, I'm pretty sure no one would enlist

But the storybooks don't really tell you
that love is a gamble,

In fact, all they really share is the
preamble


Look at it this way- love is only the
gunshot at the beginning of the race,

But once you start running you can never
be too sure what you'll face,

That's why the training is so important in
terms of working on yourself

Because every little helps in preparing for
the cards that you're dealt


But I don't want to become a cynic,

So I will believe in love even when I'm not
in it

Knowing that true love is beauty in itself
and never destroys,

I just thank God we can't all be Helen of
Troy

There are some gambles worth taking and there are some dreams worth chasing

Because sometimes taking a chance can lead to things you didn't even know you were looking for,

But when you've shut your eyes to those possibilities, it's often hard to forget there might be more

It's easy to want to play it safe but if we're being honest, that can also be boring

And also means there's so many great opportunities that we're ignoring,

So I challenge you to try something new today,

And don't let your comfortable excuses get in your way

I've recently been reflecting on trauma and
how whether or not we like to believe it,
we've all been affected by life in one way
or another

and it doesn't matter how well you've
learnt to cover them, you still have scars

Now they may not be mapped out as
clearly as the constellations of the stars but
unless you take the reins they'll always
succeed in telling you who you are


I promise this isn't me giving criticism
because I've done it all to try and cope but
in hindsight the things that constitute our
"saving" methods are never things that can
give us hope and it's safe to say that
focussing on only coping mechanisms
rather than healing strategies is a slippery
slope


The most dangerous thing we do is
interpret life from trauma instead of the
truth,

Because if the very nutrients we take in
are lies, what does that say about our fruit?

We start life with a blank canvas- crystal clear minds and consciences for us to contaminate as we go along but don't get me wrong, life in colour isn't a bad thing.

Meeting people along the way, they all help to design the life we lead so take heed for some paint darker colours than others. Some add vibrancy and excitement making you question what you think you knew and showing you who you want to be. Hold these ones near, not out of fear of losing them but rather, knowing they are dear, try to enjoy their presence whilst they're here

Then there's those who teach us pain, perhaps they're around to train us to be stronger but that doesn't dispute the fact that it hurts. We say next time we won't fall as hard, still counting scars yet maybe it's something deeper we crave... the richer the colour the more suffering endured to get there and that's only fair right? After all, it's exposure that leads to a photograph being bright

But sometimes it gets to a point where the
colours all merge into sludge and it seems
like nothing can be done to stop the art
from being condemned yet beauty is in the
eye of the beholder so you don't need
approval from all men and there may be a
masterpiece waiting to be seen by the right
person or there's someone that give you a
blank canvas and help you start again

It's always astounded me how open and
honest people can be,

I know that's something I've always
wanted to be with my poetry,

But there's a lot of hidden things that
make me the person you may see,

I guess sometimes we forget about the
roots when all we see is the tree


I think about the days when I've thought
I'd be better off dead,

Waking up every morning and being so
full of dread,

Questioning if things would be any better
if I didn't leave so much unsaid

And wondering if I have any sense of
rationality or if everything is just in my
head


It's not the easiest thing to share,

But it's worth it on the off chance that you
need to see someone on the other side of
that despair,

So I'm learning to lay myself bare,

In the hopes of reminding you that by
seeking help, you're halfway there


You see, I lost things I thought I could
never bounce back from,

And I've come further than I thought that
I could ever come,

I've fallen so many times but I've always
had at least one reason to get up,

And whether I've seen the glass as half
empty or half full, at least I've always had
a cup


So although life is complicated and it has
its ups and downs,

And there are still brief moments when I
feel like I might drown,

When all is said and done and my balance
has been found,

I've never been more grateful for when I
feel my feet firmly on the ground

I've never really been one for having
regrets, not the type who looks back at old
silhouettes,

never waiting for the next dawn once the
sun's set, but there are some things no
one's heart ever really forgets


I don't want to say that the good times
never last, or that the previous joys can
never truly be surpassed, but even if we
have to look beyond the broken heart,
sometimes comfort feels like it can only be
found in the past


And I don't often reminisce but what I'd
give to go back, despite the fact that my
heart couldn't deal with its attack, and that
the damage came with the scar tissue from
the complications I still have to unpack,
it's easy to forget that sometimes it's bad
to carry around plaques

But my new heart understands that I
won't survive if I do it all once more, that
even soldiers take rest when they've come
back from war and that I should be wiser
this time than I was before because more
harm than good will be done if I stay in
the revolving door


My new heart wants to fall back into the
rhythm of the past, but I promised myself
that last heart attack would be the last
because although before it came suddenly,
maybe this time I can make better choices,
because I wouldn't want to render the
heart surgery I underwent pointless


Maybe one day soon I'll let go and truly
start again, because what good would my
new beating heart be if on the inside I'm
dead?

Dear future me,

I hope you live to be happy waking up everyday,

And that you don't let the same obstacles keep getting in your way

I'm proud of you in advance for everything you've achieved

Even though there are so many times I didn't necessarily believe that the journey we're on would ever really lead to a destination

But we've always been destined for greatness even when we spent time wishing life would come with an explanation

We still made it against the odds

There are so many things you could have
let stop you but I'm glad you stuck it out
to see this through


And last but not least, I'm grateful that life
inspiring me, seemed to inspire you

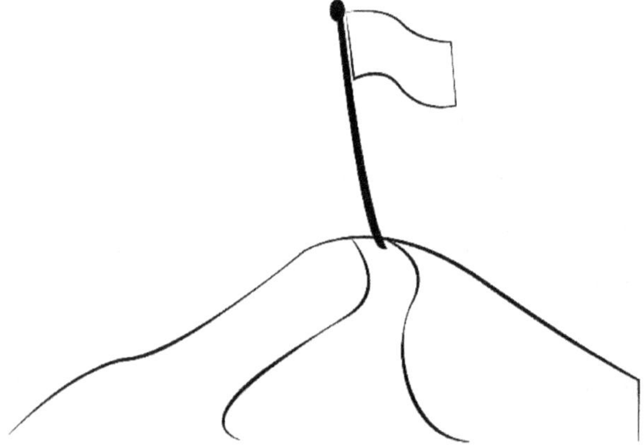

Sometimes it's really easy to look at the world and be so overwhelmed,

But in moments like these I'm reminded that it's You that's holding it all together at the helm

So with every breath that I breathe, and with every word that I speak I just want to say thank You.

And I'm not just thanking You for what You've done but for who You are and for who You continue to show Yourself to be,

So you see lockdown may have tried to shackle me but that's just made me remember that in You I'm truly free

So what comes next?

I'm not naive to the after effects

And I'm not even saying that we're through it yet

But I will say maybe the world needed this cultural reset.

Like many others this time has come to
make me truly reflect and even reconsider
so many aspects of what I previously
deemed as the norm,

And in this time I can only laugh at how
much my mind has been transformed,

So once again I say thank You.

Thank You for who You are and who You
continue to show Yourself to be,

For being the one constant in what has
been the most testing circumstances most
of us have ever seen,

And for reminding me

That You are always worthy of my
thanks, not in spite of, but especially in
moments like these

INSPIRE


Breathe in, breathe out

At a basic level that's what life is all about

Letting go of what we no longer require

Preparing for what's new is just how we're wired


Every day new opportunities arise

And in that same time we're able to get a little more wise

As if every breath was taken for a reason, just to prepare us for an upcoming season


INSPIRING


There will always be those who are able to learn from the choices we've made,

Those to show that sometimes it's okay to
be afraid

Without knowing, we can give rise to the
creation of something great

And I promise having that impact will
always be worth whatever the wait/weight


INSPIRED


And one day they'll call us inspired for the
actions we took,

But we'll get there before we reach the
epilogue of our book

For we loved with extraordinary quality
and that's the same way we lived

Knowing that like floating pollen, we
poured ourselves out on the earth and gave
all we had to give

www.ingramcontent.com/pod-product-compliance
Lightning Source LLC
LaVergne TN
LVHW021302200726
843509LV00012B/1751